1

About The Wiener Library

The Wiener Library is one of the world's leading and most extensive archives on the Holocaust and Nazi era. Formed in 1933, the Library's unique collection of over one million items includes published and unpublished works, press cuttings, photographs and eyewitness testimony.

Our vision is of a continuously developing library, archive and information service for the UK and for the international community, dedicated to supporting research, learning, teaching and advocacy about the Holocaust and genocide, their causes and consequences.

The Library provides a resource to oppose antisemitism and other forms of prejudice and intolerance. Its reputation rests on its independence and the scholarly objectivity of its activities and publications.

Our mission is:
- To serve scholars, professional researchers, the media and the public as a library of record.
- To be a living memorial to the evils of the past by ensuring that our wealth of materials is put at the service of the future.
- To engage people of all ages and backgrounds in understanding the Holocaust and its historical context through an active educational programme.
- To communicate the accessibility, power and contemporary relevance of our collections as a national resource for those wishing to prevent possible future genocides.

The Wiener Library
for the Study of the Holocaust & Genocide
29 Russell Square
London WC1B 5DP
www.wienerlibrary.co.uk

 facebook.com/wienerlibrary

@wienerlibrary

@wienerlibrary

Preface
by Dame Stephanie Shirley

From the French Protestants fleeing oppression in the 17th century, Britain has traditionally welcomed refugees, who today comprise less than 0.2% of the population. The annual Refugee Week celebrates the positive contribution that we make to society.

My personal history is as an unaccompanied five year old refugee who arrived in Britain from Vienna on the Kindertransport in 1939. Organised by Christian and Jewish activists, financially supported by the Quaker Society of Friends when it ran out of money and administered by numerous volunteers, the Kindertransport is the largest ever recorded migration of children.

The Kindertransport organised its trains from Germany, Austria, Czechoslovakia, Poland and the Free City of Danzig. Each train had about 1,000 children aged five to 16 (some small 17 year olds also snuck in) with just two adults. No limit to the permitted number of children to be rescued was ever publicly announced. Britain capped its input at 10,000 over the eight months starting December 1938. Compare this with the number of child refugees Britain talks about admitting today.

I called my foster parents Uncle and Auntie; they nurtured me as they would their own and I am their child in all but birth. Everyone told me to be grateful. Indeed I am grateful but also loved them dearly and honour their memories as I do all the Uncles and Aunties who helped us children through those terrible times.

Hitler had taken nationality away from Jewish families so I arrived Stateless and only a modicum of paperwork – the Nansen passport – formally recognised me as a displaced person registered here.

Progression was from *enemy alien* to *friendly enemy alien* and then to *friendly alien*. The shifting identity captures hate and happiness, villains and good guys. The fifth columnist or suspected terrorist, the refugee, the unwanted migrant, present a useful outlet for people's fears.

The Referendum showed that it was the fear of immigration – not immigration itself – that contributed to the Brexit decision. Contrary to expectation, regions having the highest levels of immigration were the least anxious about it.

I love this country (one of the very few that would let us children in) with a passion perhaps only someone who had lost their human rights can feel. Britain is now my home, sweet home.

As the Third Reich slips from human memory, we should always remember that genocide can only happen if local populations stand by, afraid to speak or – worse – are indifferent.

The Wiener Library honours all victims of persecution and of the genocides in Armenia, Bosnia, Cambodia, Darfur… the list goes on…

Can we not learn from these hateful experiences to love our neighbours?

Contents

Overview

Ongoing violence and upheaval in Syria, Afghanistan, Somalia, Iraq and Sudan today has created an upsurge in the number of refugees fleeing conflict, in what is commonly referred to as a refugee 'crisis'. Conflict and war, political, religious and ethnic persecution have always caused the mass displacement of populations. In Europe in the 1930s and 1940s, economic and political breakdown and the rise of extremist politics turned citizens into refugees. From 1933 and 1934, people began to leave Germany and Austria to escape political and other persecution, and after 1936, thousands more fled the Spanish Civil War and Franco's regime. Refugees also left Fascist Italy at this time.

In the late 1930s, Nazi persecution of Jews in Germany and the takeover of Austria (1938), Czechoslovakia (1938-39) and Poland (1939) produced Jewish refugees – before the Holocaust itself commenced. By 1946, war, genocide and forced population movements had created over fifty million refugees.

This exhibition examines British responses to refugees in the 1930s and 1940s. It explores governmental actions and the activities of voluntary and international organisations. It also examines the experiences of refugees themselves, including the difficulties they faced in negotiating the road to safety and in integrating into a new society.

Whilst many well-known refugees reached Britain during this period, including Sigmund Freud, here we focus on the stories of 'ordinary' people. Jews were particularly affected by the refugee crisis of the 1930s and 1940s: two thirds of Europe's Jewish population was murdered in the Holocaust. The Wiener Library was founded by Alfred Wiener, himself a German Jewish refugee, and its archives have been enriched by the collections of Jewish refugees in Britain. It is their voices and experiences that form a significant part of this exhibition.

Eva Kolmer:
'With a suitcase and a pound in my pocket'

Photograph of Eva Kolmer, then Eva Schmidt-Kolmer, after the war
© Landesarchiv Berlin

Eva Kolmer (1913-1991) was one of the approximately 30,000 Austrian Jews who came as refugees to Britain before the Second World War. From 1934-1938, most of those who left Austria were escaping political persecution.

Kolmer was a member of the Austrian Communist Party in Vienna, and she spent four months in prison after a semi-fascist regime gained power in 1934. Following the German annexation of Austria (*Anschluss*), Kolmer was advised to leave. She departed with only 'a suitcase, a ticket to Zürich and a pound in [her] pocket', and ended up in Britain, where her visa was sponsored by the editor of The Spectator magazine.

Kolmer was instrumental in establishing the Austrian Centre for Austrian refugees in London. After the November Pogrom (*Kristallnacht*) on 9-10 November 1938, the number of Jewish refugees from Austria increased, and the Austrian Centre provided crucial support. After the war, Kolmer emigrated with her husband to East Germany, where she pursued a career in paediatric medicine

Map showing the distribution of Russian and Armenian refugees after World War I. According to Russian refugee organisations, 15,000 Russian refugees came to Britain at this time. (*The Red Cross and the Refugees*, United Nations High Commissioner for Refugees)

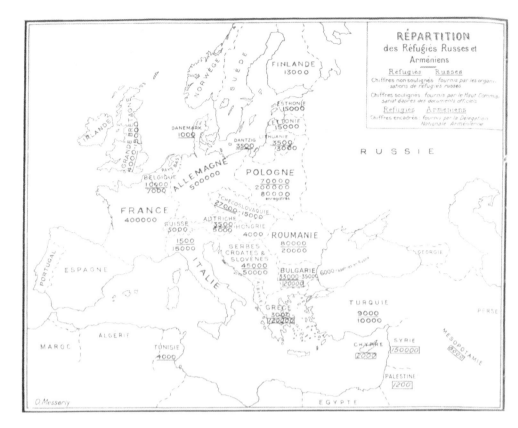

Hans Kohl's Austrian Centre membership card. The Austrian Centre provided assistance and cultural activities for several thousand refugees from Austria.

Groups of refugees arriving in Britain throughout history

1685
Tens of thousands of Huguenots (French Protestants) escaping religious persecution from 1685

Late 1800s
Tens of thousands of Russian Jews escaping pogroms after 1881

1930s-1940s
c.80,000 Jews from Nazi-controlled Europe before 1940, and other refugees, including Basque children and 5,000 political opponents to Nazism. After the war, c. 86,000 Displaced Persons (DPs)

1956-1957
Around 20,000 Hungarians during and after the Hungarian revolution

1972
27,200 Ugandan Asians expelled by Idi Amin

1980s-1990s
Over 30,000 Somalis escaping governmental collapse and civil war

2010s
In the year ending June 2016, 36,465 people applied for asylum in the UK; 9,957 people were granted asylum. Around 1,500 unaccompanied child refugees were given asylum or other form of protection, and a further 1,308 Syrians under the age of 18 were part of a resettlement scheme. The Government scheme to bring refugee children to the UK is complex and slow, and many children still await resettlement. (Source: HM Government, Immigration Statistics April to June 2016/Asylum)

A pamphlet by Violet Bonham-Carter, Child Victims of the New Germany, c.1934.

In this pamphlet, Lady Bonham-Carter highlighted the persecution that Jewish children were experiencing in schools at this early stage of Nazi rule. She urged that Jewish children from Germany be admitted into Britain. Others, such as Eleanor Rathbone, known as the 'MP for refugees', campaigned for Britain to accept large numbers of Jewish refugees. Bonham-Carter asked British people to consider how they would feel 'If It Were Your Child'.

CHILD VICTIMS OF THE NEW GERMANY

A PROTEST

By

LADY VIOLET BONHAM-CARTER.

I want to make clear my profound conviction that this is not a matter which concerns the Jewish community alone. It concerns all who believe in justice and in our common humanity. It concerns all who care for mental and spiritual freedom ; and it concerns all who care about the welfare of children and their happiness.

It is, as Lord Cecil has said, a challenge to civilization. I want to say—speaking not for myself alone, but for countless others who, like myself, though outside the Jewish community are deeply stirred by these terrible events—we wish to stand by your side in taking up this challenge.

Germany's Nightmare of Misdeeds.

I can truthfully say that nothing within my political memory has ever moved me more deeply to horror and indignation than recent events in Germany. We in this country have looked on with dazed astonishment at this nightmare. We have seen libraries burnt. We have seen monuments erected to murderers. We have seen faith and race persecuted and proscribed, thought and art forbidden unless confined in the strait-jacket of State control.

We have seen Germany banish and despoil many of her greatest and most distinguished sons, men whose high achievements in every field of endeavour have brought her honour throughout the world. And these are perhaps the happiest.

Letter from Dr Heinrich
Neuhaus to the Friends
House, London, likely
forwarded to the Inter-Aid
Committee for Children in
Oxford, 20 December 1938

Photo, Herbert Neuhaus,
undated.

VOM STAATSAMT DES INNERN
AUTORISIERTES INSTITUT FÜR MED.-KLIN. DIAGNOSTIK
Dr. med. HEINRICH NEUHAUS

WIEN, IX., GARNISONGASS
Tel. A 27-2-18

20. XII. 1938

Miss Blackhawkins
c/o Friends house
London N.W.
Dear Miss!

Excuse me the trouble made by this letter. I was told YOU can
help me. My boy is 15 years old and cannot go to England, because
nobody demanded him. The Jewish club in Vienna(I.K.G,) send
children to England, if they are demanded. I beg you instantly
help and save my boy from a great danger! The life of that
children of Jews here ist terrible.
I was a physician(specialist for bacteriologie and mikroskopie)
and I'havebeen withaut work for months. I think for myself at
last, the most impotant thing is saving of my boy.
Therefor I beg you imploringly for helping.
The datas of my boy: HERBERT NEUHAUS born in Vienna 11.9.923
frequents the Chayee-Realgymnasium(VI. year), all the school-reports
were with distiction. He plays piano about eight years, very well
and exactly. He would be able for studies in an academy of music.
His tallnis is 5,4 feet engl. The foto is enclosed.
I thank you very, very much for your kind answer and I hope it
will be successfull.
I myself was announced under the 50 phisicians for England(June 38
and I have heard nothing untill up to-day.
            Believe me, Yours very sincerely
            Dr. Heinrich NEUHAUS

P.S.
Excuse me my un-English letter
butI can not better!

Jewish parents tried every means to help their
children survive the onslaught of Nazi persecution,
including beseeching organisations for assistance.
Yet not all requests for help could be accommodated.
Dr. Heinrich Neuhaus wrote to the Friends House in
London in 1938, asking for help for his fifteen-year-
old son. Both Heinrich and his son Herbert were
deported from Vienna to Theresienstadt in November
1943. They survived and for a time, returned to
Austria. Herbert Neuhaus eventually emigrated to
the United States.

THE SITUATION OF THE REFUGEES IN SPAIN

REPORT

of the

Commission sent to Spain by the

INTERNATIONAL BUREAU FOR THE RIGHT OF ASYLUM AND AID TO POLITICAL REFUGEES

(MARCH 25 — APRIL 8, 1937)

ÉDITÉ PAR LE BUREAU INTERNATIONAL POUR LE DROIT
D'ASILE ET L'AIDE AUX REFUGIÉS POLITIQUES
10, RUE DE CHATEAUDUN, PARIS-IX

A pamphlet, *The Situation of the Refugees in Spain*, by the International Bureau for the Right of Asylum and Aid to Political Refugees, 1937.

Over 450,000 people fled Spain during the Spanish Civil War, 1936-1939. The Civil War had begun when General Franco's Nationalists attempted a military coup to overthrow the leftist government, whose forces became known as the Republicans.

Jewish families in no man's land between Hungary and Czechoslovakia in November 1938. Hundreds of people were deported into the border region by far-right nationalist Slovak militias and the Hungarian authorities. Being stranded in-between two countries without proper supplies for a week, the deportees were aided by local Jewish communities.

Deportation of Jews, Czechoslovakia, November 1938, © B. Birnbach.

Official solutions

The British Government could act entirely at its own discretion in deciding which refugees to accept in the 1930s. There was no legal concept of right of asylum, and refugees mainly attempted to enter Britain via established immigration procedures.

Before the German annexation of Austria (*Anschluss*) in 1938, border control officials determined whether political refugees or those escaping ethnic persecution could enter Britain. Refugees had to meet various criteria or be privately sponsored or self-supporting. Eligibility was not based upon the refugee's experience of persecution, and the British Government provided no funding for refugees. It was easier to obtain entry to Britain if one were wealthy or had what was deemed a 'useful' profession. Some were only allowed in on the understanding that they would settle elsewhere permanently. Others came on the *Kindertransport* scheme or as domestic servants.

After the *Anschluss*, the number of people seeking refuge in Britain increased, and in April 1938 the British Government introduced a visa system to regulate the process. Those in certain professions were often given priority. By the start of the war in 1939, Britain had given refuge to approximately 80,000 people, mostly Jews escaping Nazi oppression.

From this time, the British Government began to fund the sponsorship of refugees, but largely shut down official channels for migration from German-occupied Europe. Many refugees in Britain found their relatives were stranded. Britain blocked moves to allow more Jewish immigration to Palestine during and after the war, and also would not assure neutral countries that it would take Jewish refugees.

After the war, almost all refugees were allowed to remain permanently in Britain, and most chose to do so. The government generally recognised, in the aftermath of the Holocaust that, in the words of Sydney Silverman MP, it was cruel 'to compel [Jews] against their will, to go back to the scene of these crimes'. However, the British Government did not want to accept many more Jewish refugees. Some were permitted entry as 'domestics' or under the Home Office's Distressed Relatives Scheme. 732 Jewish child survivors, mainly boys, were also accepted, and 86,000 Displaced Persons, including many Poles, were resettled in Britain between 1947 and 1949. A minority of the admitted Displaced Persons were Jews, and some post-war DPs had been collaborators or war criminals.

It was cruel 'to compel [Jews] against their will, to go back to the scene of these crimes…'

Sydney Silverman MP

Surveillance and detention

At the start of the war, all migrants from Germany and Austria resident in Britain were subject to certain restrictions, but only Nazi sympathisers were actually interned. In the spring and summer of 1940, at a time of dramatic Nazi military successes, anti-foreign feeling and fears of enemy infiltration peaked. Following pressure from the right-wing press, around 27,000 Jewish refugees were now also interned as 'enemy aliens'. Most were released by autumn 1940. Some Jewish refugees coped relatively well with internment, whilst others, such as composer Hans Gál, found it a traumatic experience.

Photograph of internees in
Douglas, Isle of Man, 1940

The Rothschild Family: Fractured lives

Gustav Rothschild (1879-1957), a dealer in musical instruments, lived with his wife Martha (née Lindheimer, 1898-c.1942) and daughters, Trude and Edith, in Frankfurt. In November 1938, he was incarcerated in Dachau concentration camp and released on condition that he emigrate. Efforts to get a visa for the US failed, but Trude and Edith were selected for the *Kindertransport*. Gustav obtained a visa for Britain in 1939, where he was interned for a time in 1940 in the Onchan internment camp on the Isle of Man.

Martha Rothschild was supposed to follow her husband to Britain, but it proved impossible to get her out of Germany in time. Ultimately, she was deported from Frankfurt to Poland around 1942, and did not survive.

Edith Rothschild's identity document for her passage on a *Kindertransport*, 1939

Martha Rothschild.
© Yad Vashem

102/2   42170   5275

This document of identity is issued with the approval of His Majesty's Government in the United Kingdom to young persons to be admitted to the United Kingdom for educational purposes under the care of the Inter-Aid Committee for children.

THIS DOCUMENT REQUIRES NO VISA.

PERSONAL PARTICULARS.

Name ROTHSCHILD EDITH

Sex FEMALE   Date of Birth 21.11.25

Place FRANKFURT

Full Names and Address of Parents

ROTHSCHILD GUSTAV & MARTHA

FURSTENBERGERSTR 167

FRANKFURT a/M.

COPY/

UNIVERSAL COVERS LTD.

Telephone)
Telegrams) Langside 1635
Glasgow.

Universal Works,
40, Coustonholm Road,
Pollokshaws,
Glasgow, S.3.

3rd December, 1938.

Messrs. Gilbert Samuel & Co.,
6, Great Winchester Street,
London, E.C.2.

Dear Sirs,

I have your letter of 2nd December regarding the guarantee
for Mr. Gustav Rothschild.

I would have liked if this guarantee could be limited to
an amount, say £200, and if this is possible I would be glad
if you would arrange it so.   If not, then I will proceed with
it as it stands.   When Mr. Fritz Rothschild wrote to me to
ask if I would be willing to sign this guarantee he informed
me that a brother-in-law of Mr. Gustav Rothschild, namely Mr.
Oppenheimer, would be willing to give me a counter guarantee
on the same lines as the one I must give to the Aid Committee.
Will you please therefore inform Mr. Rothschild that, as soon
as I receive this counter guarantee, I will complete mine.

I would be glad if with this counter guarantee, I could
have the full name, address, age, and details regarding the
business carried on and the amount of income which is derived
and also a banker's reference or the name of his bankers.

I have undertaken in all to guarantee for three separate
individuals and, while I am financially able to support such
guarantees, I must satisfy my own bankers that I am not doing so
in a reckless manner, and I do not care to ask my bankers for
a certificate without providing them with the information which
I am asking you to get from Mr. Oppenheimer.   I will do
whatever is required without any unnecessary delay as soon as
I have these particulars from you.

                    Yours faithfully,

                        JOSEPH L. LEVY

Letter relating to the sponsorship of Gustav Rothschild, which
enabled him to obtain a visa for Britain, 1938

GERMAN JEWISH AID COMMITTEE

IMMIGRATION SECTION

52, BEDFORD WAY,

LONDON, W.C.1.

6th March, 1939

Our Ref: EAF/FF

Mr.Gustav Rothschild,
148, Fuerstenbergerstrasse,
Frankfurt a.Main.

Dear Sir / Madam,

We have pleasure in advising you that you
through the nearest British Consul
should apply for a visa/to the British Passport Control

Officer in Berlin to whom a communication has been

sent by the Home Office.

Your reference No is R.11140.

Yours faithfully,

GERMAN JEWISH AID COMMITTEE.

ON ARRIVAL IN GREAT BRITAIN YOU SHOULD
REPORT EITHER IN PERSON OR BY LETTER TO
BLOOMSBURY HOUSE, BLOOMSBURY STREET,
LONDON. W.C.1.

Please address ALL communications to the Committee and NOT to individuals.

Letter to Gustav Rothschild advising that he could apply for a visa, 1939

Neue

kritische

Besprechungen

JOHANNA BEHREND

Lieder- und Oratoriensängerin

(Sopran)

Johanna Behrend (1892-1977) was born in Berlin in a Jewish household but later converted to Christianity. She studied music and became a concert singer and later a secretary. As a person of Jewish origin, she was dismissed from her job in November 1938 and in 1939 came to England as a refugee. Behrend initially worked in Brighton as a domestic servant with friends of her family.

Central Police Station,

Town Hall,

Brighton, 1.

9th October, 1939

To   Johanna Dorothea Sara BEHREND,
      11, Shirmley Road,
      Hove.

Tribunals have been appointed by the Secretary of State to examine the position of all Germans and Austrians over the age of 16 in this country, and to consider which of them can properly be exempted from internment and which of those exempted from intern- ment can be exempted also from the special restrictions which are imposed by the Aliens Order on enemy aliens, i.e. the restrictions on travelling without a travel permit, on change of residence withoutthe permission of the police, and on the possession without a police permit of certain articles including motor cars, cameras, etc.

Your case will be considered by the tribunal sitting at the Royal Pavilion, Brighton and you should attend there on Saturday   14th October, 1939   at 11.45 a.m. .   You should bring with you your Police Registration Certificate.

If you are well-known to a British subject or to someone who has lived here a long time or are in the employment of such person, you should ask such person to state in writing what he or she knows about you, and you should send the statement to me as soon as possible. You can also invite such a person to attend in case the tribunal wants to put any questions to him or her.

Legal representatives (solicitors or barristers) will not be allowed to act as advocates before the tribunal.

If you are unable to attend in accordance with this notice, you should send me without delay a statement in writing explaining the reason.

C.J.Forward.

Chief Inspector,
Secretary,
Aliens Tribunal,
Brighton Area.

Letter from the Chief Inspector of the Aliens Tribunal, Brighton Area, to Johanna Behrend, 9 October 1939, summoning Behrend to a tribunal to determine whether she should be interned as an Austrian or German 'alien'.

In the summer of 1940, c.2,500 Austrian and German internees were sent to Australia aboard the *Dunera*. Around four-fifths of the internees were political refugees and refugees of Jewish origin. Conditions on board the ship were dire, and brutality and theft by the British guards common. Once in Australia, the Jewish refugees were interned at Hay Camp, New South Wales. They were released after the Pearl Harbor attack, and most made their way back to Britain and served in the British Armed Forces.

Currency used in Hay internment camp, Australia, 1941.

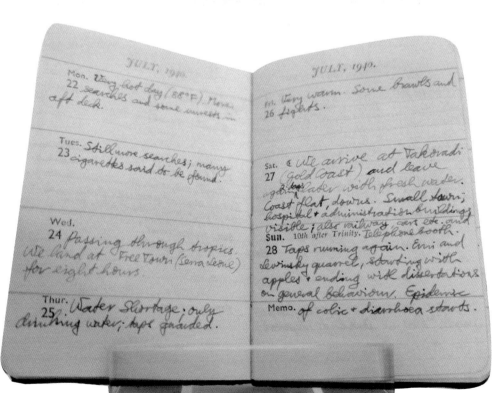

Photo of Bernard (Bernd) Simon as a boy, with pages from his diary written aboard HMT *Dunera* (1940)

Certificate No. **AZ** 39876   Home Office No. S. 22292.

BRITISH NATIONALITY AND STATUS OF ALIENS ACT, 1914

CERTIFICATE OF NATURALIZATION

Whereas   Elise Steiner

has applied to one of His Majesty's Principal Secretaries of State for a Certificate of Naturalization, alleging with respect to   herself the particulars set out below, and has satisfied him that the conditions laid down in the above-mentioned Act for the grant of a Certificate of Naturalization are fulfilled in **her** case :

Now, therefore, in pursuance of the powers conferred on him by the said Act, the Secretary of State grants to the said

         Elise Steiner

this Certificate of Naturalization, and declares that upon taking the Oath of Allegiance within the time and in the manner required by the regulations made in that behalf she shall, subject to the provisions of the said Act, be entitled to all political and other rights, powers and privileges, and be subject to all obligations, duties and liabilities, to which a natural-born British subject is entitled or subject, and have to all intents and purposes the status of a natural-born British subject.

In witness whereof I have hereto subscribed my name this 3rd   day of

March, 1948

Under Secretary of State.

HOME OFFICE,
LONDON.

PARTICULARS RELATING TO APPLICANT

Full Name	Elise STEINER.
Address	Washington Hall Training College for Teachers, Euxton, Chorley, Lancashire.
Trade or Occupation	Student.
Place and date of birth	Vienna, Austria. 14th April, 1923.
Nationality	Austrian.
Single, married, etc.	Single.
Name of wife or husband	- - -
Names and nationality of parents	Hermann and Johanna STEINER. (Austrian)

(For Oath
see overleaf)

22

Elise Steiner was born into an Orthodox Jewish family in Vienna in 1923. Her uncle was able to fund a year's stay in a British boarding school, and Steiner left Austria on a *Kindertransport* in November 1938. She did not see the rest of her immediate family again, as they perished during the Holocaust. After the war, Steiner remained in Britain to study child development, and later became a university lecturer in early childhood education. She died in London in 2010.

Letter from 2005 showing that Elise Steiner received 1,000 Euros compensation for the loss of family property during the Nazi era. Her parents had owned a small stationery shop.

The following information is enclosed for your convenience,
should you prefer reading English

Vienna, Feber 18, 2005
2b

Dear Sir/Madam,

you have received the lump-sum payment of 7.630 EURO / 7.000 USD from the **National Fund of the Republic of Austria for Victims of National Socialism** as compensation for losses of property in the categories *apartment and small business leases, household property and personal valuables* according to § 2b National Fund Law BGBl. I Nr. 11/2001 in the valid version.

§ 2b National Fund Law provides that the remaining amount will be distributed in equal parts among all persons entitled to benefits or their heirs respectively.

For this reason it is our pleasure to be able to inform you that the Board of Trustees of the National Fund of Austria for Victims of National Socialism has decided upon

a payment of the amount of 1.000,00 Euro

(in letters one thousand Euro)

as a final additional payment to you.

This amount will be remitted in the next eight to ten weeks in the form declared by you.

We are conscious of the fact that the injustice that you and your family have been subjected to can not be made up for. Yet, we close with the deep hope that through its work, the National Fund has succeeded in expressing the efforts towards a reconciliation rendered by the Republic of Austria.

Respectfully yours,

President of the National Council   Secretary General
Dr. Andreas Khol e.h.   Mag. Hannah M. Lessing e.h.

23

International responses

The refugee crisis generated by the First World War and the Russian Revolution and civil war provoked an international response.

International organisations, such as the Red Cross and later the League of Nations (set up in 1919), were established in response to the plight of millions of people who found themselves displaced by war and its chaotic aftermath. In 1921, the League of Nations created the High Commissioner for Refugees, led by Norwegian Fridtjof Nansen. Nansen persuaded the international community to agree to the issue of 'Nansen Passports' for stateless people. Many other voluntary international organisations assisted refugees and raised awareness of their circumstances.

British Red Cross Society
Staff in Occupied Germany

'Who is a genuine, bona fide and deserving refugee?'

1950 Iro manual for eligibility office

Refugees, International Organisations and the Second World War

In July 1938, an inter-governmental summit to discuss the plight of Jewish refugees from Germany, held in Évian, France, failed to reach an agreement. The Second World War left a vast number of refugees in its wake, and in 1943, the United Nations Relief and Rehabilitation Agency (UNRRA) was founded to respond. The organisation, which included 44 member countries, attempted to help Displaced Persons (DPs) in Europe with humanitarian aid and determined eligibility for assistance. Working alongside military authorities, UNRRA helped thousands of DPs with resettlement and repatriation, and by the start of 1946, three quarters of DPs had returned home. Around twelve million ethnic Germans who lived in Central and Eastern Europe and who were expelled after the war had become refugees, but were not eligible for assistance.

In DP camps and urban centres in the Allied zones of occupation, UNRRA provided relief to survivors of Nazi persecution and other displaced people, although policies in the British zone prevented Jews from being defined as a distinct category for assistance. Within the context of the brewing Cold War, by 1947 UNRRA's priorities shifted. Being anti-Communist became a crucial determinant of whether people were deemed eligible for UNRRA's help. Some wartime perpetrators from the Baltic states and Yugoslavia were assisted by UNRRA with resettlement at this time if they could prove they were sufficiently anti-communist. In July 1947, the International Refugee Organisation (IRO) took over UNRRA's work.

The Red Cross (founded 1863) provided refugees during and after the war with food, shelter and medicine, and helped families separated by persecution and war to remain in contact. The Red Cross, UNRRA and its successor, the IRO, helped trace and reunite surviving relatives, efforts that coalesced into the establishment of the International Tracing Service. The 1951 United Nations Refugee Convention defined the term 'refugee' and legally codified practises of granting asylum that had been in existence for some time.

Refugees to Britain and International Organisations

In the 1930s and 1940s, many refugees who came to Britain were helped by international organisations. After the war, UNRRA helped channel some DPs into the European Voluntary Workers (EVW) scheme, which supplied often lowly-paid workers to sectors of the economy with labour shortages. Most of those helped by this scheme were not Jews, but Lithuanians, Latvians and Ukrainians, including some who had served in the Waffen-SS.

A.E.F. D.P. REGISTRATION RECORD
Original ☒   Duplicate ☐

(1) REGISTRATION NO. | 5 0 3 5 7 0 7 | For coding purposes | A. B. C. D. E. F. G. H. I. J.

M. ☒ Single ☒   Married ☐
F. ☐ Widowed ☐   Divorced ☐

Dr Wirth   Stefan

(2) Family Name	Other Given Names	(3) Sex	(4) Marital Status	(5) Claimed Nationality
				Hungarian Jew

4. 2. 1916.   Budapest   Hungary   Israelit

(6) Birthdate	Birthplace	Province	Country	(7) Religion (Optional)	(8) Number of Accompanying Family Members:

(9) Number of Dependents:

Wirth Kálmán   Krausz Zoltán

(10) Full Name of Father	(11) Full Maiden Name of Mother

(12) DESIRED DESTINATION	(13) LAST PERMANENT RESIDENCE OR RESIDENCE JANUARY 1, 1938
Palestine	Budapest Hungary
City or Village Province Country	City or Village Province Country

advocat

(14) Usual Trade, Occupation or Profession	(15) Performed in What Kind of Establishment	(16) Other Trades or Occupations

Hungarian, German, English

(17) Languages Spoken in Order of Fluency	(18) Do You Claim to be a Prisoner of War	(19) Amount and Kind of Currency in your Possession
a. b. c.	Yes No	

(20) Signature of Registrant: Dr Stefan Wirth

(21) Signature of Registrar: Schwarz Stefan   Date: 20.3.1946

Assembly Center No. 905

(22) Destination or Reception Center: D.P. Sanatorium   Gauting.   UNRRA   Hospital   Team 905

Name or Number	City or Village	Province	Country

(23) Code for Issue | 1 | 2 | 3 | 4 | 5 | 6 | 7 | 8 | 9 | 10 | 11 | 12 | 13 | 14 | 15 | 16 | 17 | 18 | 19 | 20 | 21 | 22 | 23 | 24 | 25 | 26 | 27 | 28 |

(24) REMARKS

K.Z. No Dachau 151798.   Certificate No 5206.

DP-2

István Wirth:
Displaced, and displaced again

István (later Stephen) Wirth (1916–1982), a Hungarian Jew from Budapest, reached an UNRRA centre near Munich after surviving two concentration camps, slave labour and a death march. For two years, he recovered in hospital. Wirth's father and two of his three brothers died in the Holocaust. In 1947, he returned to Budapest, earned a PhD and worked as a lawyer and a judge. He married Éva, an Auschwitz survivor, who became a statistician in the Prime Minister's office. Encountering a rise in antisemitism at the start of the Hungarian Uprising in 1956, Wirth fled Hungary with his three-year-old son, David, leaving Éva behind with their baby son László. They were refugees in Austria before coming to Britain. In London, Wirth opened a market stall and for many years, his family relied on charity to get by.

Dr Wirth's DP Registration Record © ITS Digital Archive, Wiener Library

In order to join her husband, István, and their young son, David, in Britain, Éva Wirth had to renounce her Hungarian citizenship to obtain an exit visa in 1957. She was thus stateless as she made her way across Europe via Yugoslavia and Italy with their other son, László, who was then a baby. Éva was reunited with her husband and older son in Britain. Éva, who had been a statistician, worked in Britain as a night cook at a hospital and helped with her husband's market stall during the day.

The travel document of Éva Wirth, 1957 © David Wirth.

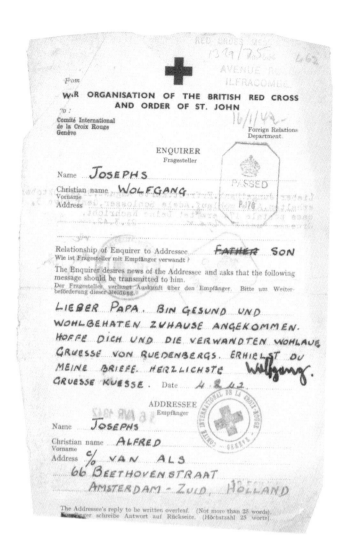

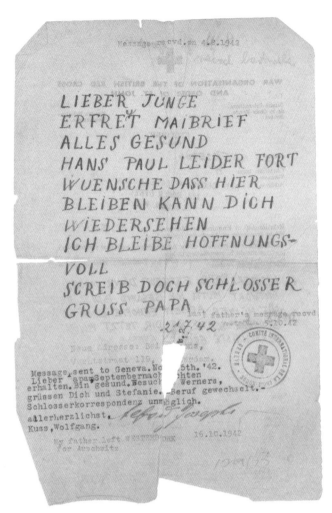

The Red Cross was able to help separated families keep in touch during the war by transmitting short messages via neutral countries, such as Portugal. Wolfgang Josephs was a German Jew who first came to Britain in July 1933. By the late 1930s, his father, Alfred, lived in Amsterdam. Josephs was interned as an 'enemy alien' at the outbreak of war and later transported on the *Dunera* to Hay Internment Camp, Australia. On Josephs' return to Britain in 1941 he enlisted in the Pioneers Corps and changed his name to Peter Johnson.

Red Cross telegrams from Alfred Josephs to his son, Wolfgang (also known as Peter Johnson), including the last message Wolfgang received from his father.

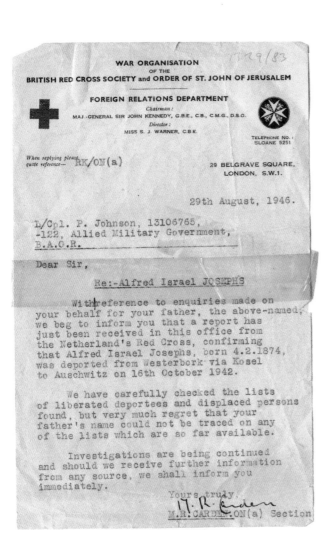

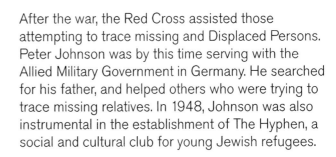

After the war, the Red Cross assisted those attempting to trace missing and Displaced Persons. Peter Johnson was by this time serving with the Allied Military Government in Germany. He searched for his father, and helped others who were trying to trace missing relatives. In 1948, Johnson was also instrumental in the establishment of The Hyphen, a social and cultural club for young Jewish refugees.

Letter from the British Red Cross Society to Peter Johnson, previously Wolfgang Josephs, about his search for his father Alfred, 29 August 1946.

Wolfgang Josephs (Peter Johnson) with his father Alfred, on holiday in Allgäu Hohenschwangau, Bavaria, 1920.

INSTRUCTIONS FOR REPLY

FR/CL./29b

TO ANSWER THIS MESSAGE—

(a) You may write up to 25 words on purely personal and family matters on the back of the enclosed Red Cross Message form. Place it in an envelope addressed to—

Comité International de la Croix-Rouge,
Palais du Conseil Général,
Geneva, Switzerland.

Mark your envelope clearly on the front "Red Cross Postal Message Scheme", and post it in the ordinary way (3d. stamp or 5d. air mail).

NO ADDRESS, OR CHANGE OF ADDRESS, MAY BE GIVEN WHEN REPLYING ON THE BACK OF THE ENCLOSED MESSAGE FORM.

If you have changed your address, take or post the enclosed message, with your reply written on the back, to your nearest Red Cross Message Bureau, which will despatch it and record your new address for you. You should take a stamped (3d. stamp) envelope with you to the Bureau addressed as above.

[P.T.O.

(b) If you wish to keep the enclosed Red Cross Message, you may go to a Red Cross Message Bureau, which is generally at a Citizens' Advice Bureau, and send a fresh message. This will cost 1/-.

THE ADDRESS OF YOUR NEAREST BUREAU CAN BE OBTAINED FROM THE POST OFFICE

N.B.—WHEN REPLYING TO THIS MESSAGE—

(1) **Do not** mention or hint about Service matters. Even such remarks as "Tom in Army", "Jack gone East", "Bill near where we spent holiday in 1938", etc., will not be passed by the Censor.

(2) **Do not** mention the receipt of "Radio Messages", "Letters", or "Cards". Some non-committal phrase such as "Received your message, or news" should be used.

(3) **Do not** mention results of enemy action.

(4) **Do not** mention names of towns.

(5) **Do not** suggest corresponding through an intermediary or any means other than through the Red Cross.

(6) **Do not** cross out anything that you write on the form.

S & D Ltd—15632

30

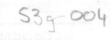

A Program

on

United Nations Relief and Rehabilitation

Based on a one-day conference of 50 national women's organizations convened at the Mayflower Hotel, Washington, D. C., 20 October 1944, by the Women's Conference on International Affairs. Published by the United Nations Relief and Rehabilitation Administration, 1344 Conn. Ave., Washington, D. C.

Washington, D. C.
1944

Pamphlet excerpt, A Program on United Nations Relief and Rehabilitation (UNRRA), published in Washington DC, 1940s.

This section of the pamphlet discusses the work of the UNRRA Displaced Persons programme. It emphasises that UNRRA sought, so far as possible, to facilitate the organised return of people to their countries of origin. Although many people were repatriated, many Jewish survivors did not want to return, and post-war, Communist rule in Eastern Europe made return difficult or impossible for others. Later, under the auspices of the International Refugee Organisation (IRO), the focus switched to resettlement rather than return.

My brother's keeper

Before the Second World War, Anglo-Jewish Communities intervened in response to the plight of Jews in Germany, even whilst facing domestic concerns, including increasing antisemitism.

Following the Nazi boycott of Jewish-owned businesses in April 1933, a delegation of prominent representatives from the Board of Deputies of British Jews and the Anglo-Jewish Association, amongst others, asked the Home Secretary for a generous response to a possible influx of Jewish refugees. The Anglo-Jewish community created a framework for coordinating its responses and financially supporting Jewish refugees in Britain.

Jewish organisations tried to respond efficiently, although they had different aims and, not infrequently, opposing views on how to achieve them. They raised funds, prepared refugees for emigration to Britain, and assisted them once they arrived with legal, education and health and social welfare services. Some 80,000 Jewish refugees arrived in Britain by the late 1930s, including about 20,000 women as domestic servants and around 10,000 children on the *Kindertransport*. Others emigrated through a variety of means, including through sponsors and professional connections

VISA DE TRANSIT.

Nom du bénéficiaire: Charlotte Pilpel

Nationalité: Allem...

Visé sous le no 4064 au Consulat Général de Belgique à Vienne, pour permettre au titulaire du présent passeport de transiter par la Belgique. -

Avis important: Il est interdit au bénéficiaire de de visa de s'arrêter volontairement en Belgique ou de s'y établir.

Vienne, le 29. April 1939

Pour le Consul Général de Belgique:

PILPEL Charlotte

VISA FOR UNITED KINGDOM
Date 27. APR. 1939 No K 68931
GRANTED at VIENNA
SIG.
BRITISH PASSPORT CONTROL OFFICER
GOOD FOR SINGLE JOURNEY ONLY

Valid for entry to U.K. within 90 days
Granted under instructions "Re
PARAGRAPH 13

D. 5045

For domestic employment.

LEAVE TO LAND GRANTED AT DOVER THIS DAY ON CONDITION THAT THE HOLDER REGISTERS AT ONCE WITH THE POLICE AND DOES NOT ENTER ANY EMPLOYMENT OTHER THAN AS A RESIDENT IN SERVICE IN A PRIVATE HOUSEHOLD.

The passport of Charlotte Smith (née Pilpel) with visa stamps for the UK. Pilpel's parents were unable to emigrate from Vienna and were murdered during the Holocaust.

Refugee Resettlement Farm Millisle, County Down, N. Ireland, 1939 or early 1940s. Operating from 1938 to 1948, the farm was home to dozens of refugees, who were supported by the Belfast Jewish community, Central British fund and the Joint Christian Churches.

At the Jewish Refugee Committee's offices in Woburn House, where Bloomsbury House was moved, late 1930s

Refugee Organisations

The Central British Fund for German Jewry (CBF) raised millions of pounds for the Jewish Refugee Committee (JRC, also known as the German Jewish Aid Committee) and other groups to support refugees. Founded in October 1933, the JRC assisted Jewish refugees with housing, medical care, and training. The Refugee Children's Movement (RCM) helped organise the emigration and resettlement of Jewish children selected for the *Kindertransport* after the Government agreed to waive visa requirements for those sponsored by the Children's Inter-Aid Committee. The RCM worked alongside B'nai B'rith and the Women's International Zionist Federation and other groups, such as the Quakers. The Chief Rabbi's Religious Emergency Council, led by Rabbi Solomon Schonfeld, organised transports of children, rabbis, *shochets* (ritual slaughterers) and teachers to Britain, and settled them in Orthodox communities. The Lord Baldwin Fund, Council for German Jewry and British ORT also supported refugees. The Academic Assistance Council (later, Council for At-Risk Academics, CARA), founded in 1933 by William Beveridge, assisted academics that were forced to flee Nazi Germany.

Refugees Helping Refugees

Not all Jewish refugees who came to Britain benefited from the assistance of an aid organisation. This resulted in the creation of networks of support by refugees, for refugees. Founded in 1941, the Association of Jewish Refugees (AJR) strove 'to represent all the Jewish refugees from Germany for whom Judaism was a determining factor in their outlook on life'. The AJR provided legal and social services, and it worked to build political will for the acceptance of Jewish refugees in Britain after the war. The AJR organised meetings and published information for members in the AJR Information (later AJR Journal). With support from the CBF, it created the first homes for elderly refugees and survivors. The AJR became the 'voice' of German-speaking Jewish refugees, and in time, counted Jewish refugees and survivors from across Europe amongst its members.

Jewish refugees organised mutual aid associations and social clubs around professions, culture, religious communities and other interests, some of which were coordinated by the AJR. For instance, the AJR supported The Hyphen, which was a group established in 1948 by Peter Johnson (Wolfgang Josephs, see p30) for younger Jewish refugees.

Refugee assistance: Charlotte Lewin

Charlotte Lewin lived and worked in Breslau as an English and French teacher. She held various positions, including Secretary at the American Consulate, and at archives and libraries in Breslau. In October 1936, Lewin was imprisoned for making defamatory remarks about Nazi Minister of Propaganda Joseph Goebbels when he came to Breslau. After her release, she wanted to leave, and managed to reach Britain in March 1938. She was employed as a German language teacher for HM Forces, and worked tirelessly on behalf of her family and friends to help them navigate the bureaucratic hurdles required to leave Breslau.

71, Goldhurst Terrace,
London, N.W.6.
10.12.1938

Dear Mr. Jourdan:

Forgive me for troubling you again after your last letter. But I have had news which you will see is more favourable. Friends in the United States have sent an affidavit for Dr. and Mrs.Hirsch-Kauffmann, but this must take a little time, presumably a few months to come into action. The Quakers have promised to give them hospitality for that time, so if you will be so kind as to help your relative to come over, your responsibility would be very slight. If not the chances are that she will be seperated from her husband according to the new laws and be destitute and miserable.

I beg of you as a Christian man and of your humanity to help your relative. She and her husband are worthy people. That I can guarantee. And your responsibility, as I have already mentioned, would only be slight and for a short time until one can get them over to the United States. Their fares to England and to America would be paid in Germany, that it would cost you no money at all. But the English Government requires that a British subject, preferably a relative, should sign the guarantee.

I pray you of your charity to give your help.

Yours faithfully,

Letter from Charlotte Lewin to one Mr Jourdan on behalf of
friends Dr and Mrs Hirsch Kaufmann

Government Grant

CENTRAL COMMITTEE FOR REFUGEES.
Chairman: Sir Herbert Emerson.
Secretary: Mr. F.E. Bendit.

Co-Ordinating all Committees.

CENTRAL OFFICE FOR REFUGEES.
Joint Chairmen: Rev. Henry Carter & Mr. Anthony de Rothschild.
Secretary: Miss I. Charlesworth.

Fund Raising.	Co-Ordinating Regional Refugee Councils .	Fund Raising.
CHRISTIAN COUNCIL FOR REFUGEES. Chairman of Board of Management: Rev. Henry Carter. Secretary: Miss M. Karpeles.	PROVINCIAL DEPARTMENT. Chairman: Mr. Otto M. Schiff. Secretary: Miss Joan Stiebel.	CENTRAL COUNCIL FOR JEWISH REFUGEES. Chairman: Mr. Anthony de Rothschild. Secretary: Mr. Myer Stephany.
Case Working	Case Working	Case Working
FRIENDS COMMITTEE ON REFUGEES AND ALIENS. Chairman: Mr. H. Rowntree. Secretary: Miss B. Bracey.	CHURCH OF ENGLAND COMMITTEE. Chairman: Bishop of Chichester. Secretary: Miss H. Roberts.	REFUGEE CHILDRENS MOVEMENT LTD. Chairman: Lord Gorrel. Secretary: Mrs. D.H. Hardisty.	JEWISH REFUGEES COMMITTEE. Jt. Chairmen: Mr. Otto M. Schiff. Mr. Leslie B. Prince. Jt. Secretaries: Miss Ruth Fellner. Miss Joan Stiebel.

'Every Wednesday afternoon I met Bina, and we went by underground to Bloomsbury House. The great building had been a hotel. Here and there stucco was breaking away and there were cracks in the walls. No one worried about these signs of decay because it housed our future hopes....Bina and I took numbers and joined the large queue besieging the offices. The faces of many of those stranded here in the waiting hall of bureaucracy reflected the misery of exile, which, except for their mere existence, had deprived them of everything that had once given them pleasure and a place in life. For the mercy of mere physical survival, they were dispossessed, humiliated and uprooted. It often took hours until we were admitted to a large office and approached one of the dozen or so desks there.'

From *Salo's Song*, Barbara Esser

Table showing the Main Committees in Bloomsbury House, c. 1943.

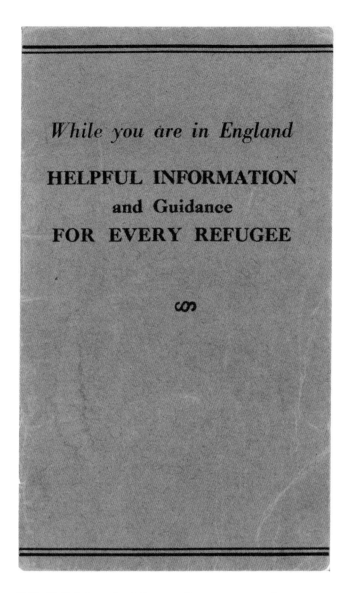

While you are in England

HELPFUL INFORMATION
and Guidance
FOR EVERY REFUGEE

∽

The
TOLERANCE AND SYMPATHY
of Britain and the British Commonwealth

THE traditional tolerance and sympathy of Britain and the British Commonwealth towards the Jews is something which every British Jew appreciates profoundly. On his part he does all in his power to express his loyalty to Britain and the British Commonwealth, in word and in deed, by personal service and by communal effort.

This loyalty comes first and foremost, and every Refugee should realise how deeply it is felt.

The Jewish Community in Britain will do its very utmost to welcome and maintain all Refugees, to educate their Children, to care for the Aged and the Sick—and to assist in every possible way in creating new homes for them overseas. A great many Christians, in all walks of life, have spontaneously associated themselves with this work. All that we ask from you in return is to carry out to your utmost the following lines of conduct. Regard them, please, as **duties to which you are in honour bound :**

Page 10

With Britain's entry into war, the presence of refugees in Britain was called further into question, particularly that of the tens of thousands who were considered 'enemy aliens' and interned in camps. Attempting to strike a balance between national interests in wartime and the needs of refugees, the JRC published this bilingual pamphlet. The pamphlet implores its reader: 'Spread courage by word and deed. There is a new and better future before you! Be loyal to England, your host.'

While You are in England: Helpful Information and Guidance for Every Refugee, Pamphlet published by the German Jewish Aid Committee and the Board of Deputies, c. 1938.

The Association of Jewish Refugees (AJR), founded in 1941, provided a vital means for Jewish refugees to connect to each other, staving off the loneliness and loss many refugees and survivors experienced having left their homes, livelihoods and families behind. All AJR members received a monthly journal, which included news analysis, feature articles, as well as book, theatre and film reviews. The AJR continues to publish the information today as the *AJR Journal*.

AJR Information, Issue No. 5, May 1946.

No. 5

MAY 1946

AJR INFORMATION

ISSUED BY THE
ASSOCIATION OF JEWISH REFUGEES IN GREAT BRITAIN
8, FAIRFAX MANSIONS, LONDON, N.W.3

Office and Consulting Hours: 10 a.m.—1 p.m., 3—6 p.m., Sunday 10 a.m.—1 p.m.
Telephone: MAIda Vale 9096

DISCUSSION ON REFUGEES

WHILE we are going to press, delegates from 22 countries, and observers on behalf of the Inter-Governmental Committee on Refugees and of UNRRA respectively discuss the legal and political protection, rehabilitation, and final resettlement of refugees and displaced persons. They form the special committee which has been set up by direction of the General Assembly of UNO to deal with that intricate complex of problems.

The unambiguous and clear definition of the term "refugee" presented one of the greatest initial difficulties. The definition was by no means a formality but a political factor par excellence. The proposal of the British delegate that the term "refugee" should also apply to persons who left their country because they were out of sympathy with the regime in force there, was bound to meet with the opposition of the Russian, Polish, Ukrainian and Yugoslav representatives. As already outlined on a previous occasion, many of the displaced persons from those countries had volunteered for the Nazi war machine and are Nazi sympathisers.

According to the proposal of the Inter-Governmental Committee, the term "refugee" should be applied to persons who left their country of nationality or residence because of fear or danger to their lives and liberty on account of race, religion or political belief. The proposal, introduced by Sir Herbert Emerson, suggests that three groups of refugees should come under the protection of any Inter-Governmental body set up for this purpose by the United Nations, viz., all those who were refugees at the beginning of the second World War, those who had become refugees during that war, and any other categories which the Inter-Governmental body may include in the future.

The principle submitted by the delegates of the U.S.A. and the U.K. that no one should be forced to return to his country of origin against his or her will, will no doubt be upheld although some categories may be encouraged to go back. It was said not without emphasis that some time ago the respective countries did not want their refugees; now the refugees did not want their countries.

A serious shortcoming, more: a lacking sense of reality may develop by the committee's refusal to recognise the existence of Jewish D.P.'s as a group and species of their own. At present, this neglect may not have any practical consequences as the Anglo-American Commission on Palestine has been charged with investigating the position of Jewish displaced persons and is soon to report on its findings.

CONTRIBUTION TO SCIENCE

REFUGEES have been subjected to much unfair and ignorant criticism. All the more laudable that the *Manchester Guardian*, in a leading article, recalls some of their outstanding merits. The occasion is a review of "Science and Victory," a pamphlet referred to on another page of this issue. It emphasises that one result of the purge of the universities with which the Nazis "celebrated" their seizure of power in 1933, was that "the benefit to be had from exploiting brains which should have been the enemy's has never been enjoyed on such a scale by a country at war as by America and ourselves in the last few years."

"If there was to be ' prejudiced ' criticism of our refugees," the *Manchester Guardian* concludes, "they may well ask that some of the grounds for favourable prejudice should not be overlooked."

THE FIRST FIVE YEARS

The Annual General Meeting held on April 25 at Stern Hall, London, marked the completion of five years' activities of the AJR. From the day in 1941 when nine men came together and decided to handle the affairs of Jewish refugees from Germany and Austria in Great Britain, a long and thorny path has led up to the place the Association now occupies in Jewish life in this country. It enjoys the confidence of the authorities who are dealing with refugee questions, and has established close contact with kindred organisations abroad.

The outstanding event for refugees in Great Britain during the year under review was the resumption of naturalisation. Even if many will have to wait a considerable time until they will become British subjects, the barriers which have hitherto blocked the way to legal absorption are removed. Anxieties that people might be compelled to leave their country of refuge have been dispelled. However, we know that movements are at work who propagate anti-alien sentiment, and we have to be on the alert.

A great number of refugees who had to change over to new trades and professions, have attained a firm place in the economic life of this country either as employers or employees. On the other hand, the transition from war to peace brings forth new and difficult problems. Ex-servicemen, who had no occupation before joining up, must be absorbed in the economic life as well as others who have lost their war jobs. The AJR in time completed the necessary preparatory work which now can be turned into practical help.

With the end of the war the mournful balance of the remnants of Continental Jewry had to be drawn, and help for the survivors became the foremost aim of the AJR. The Clothing Collection, originally a temporary measure, has developed into a permanent and blessed undertaking. The Transmare scheme, a search action established some years ago, succeeded in putting hundreds of people in touch with each other ; it also had the distressing task of informing many refugees of the death of their relatives or friends. As a member of the " Joint Committee for Jews in Germany," the AJR shares in the work of improving the grave position of the Jews in Germany. Personal contacts with Jews on the Continent have again been established, both by visits of representatives of the AJR to Germany and other countries, and by visits of representatives of Continental Jewries to London.

Tens of thousands of Jews on the Continent are in need of new homes and for most of them Palestine will be the only congenial country. The AJR welcomed it warmly that it had the opportunity of putting this point of view before the Anglo-American Enquiry Commission in written as well as in oral evidence.

Realising that the tremendous tasks lying ahead cannot be accomplished by any single organisation or any individual, the AJR was instrumental in forming a union with the organisations of refugees from Germany in all countries of the world—the " Council for the Protection of the Rights and Interests of Jews from Germany." Owing to the fact that the management of the Council is connected with the AJR, and that its President, Rabbi Dr. Leo Baeck, is in closest contact with the Executive Committee of the AJR, our organisation has been assigned a special part in this work. Restitution and reparation is one of the problems to which the Council devotes itself.

The AJR co-operates with the leading Jewish organisations in this country and with the international bodies in charge of refugee questions, above all the " Inter-Governmental Committee on Refugees." Our political friends are always prepared to assist us whenever necessary and knowing the importance of public opinion, we have also established good relations with the Press. " AJR Information," though still in its initial stages, has already met with good response.

As for the future, we know that with the legal absorption of the refugees the tasks of the AJR will by no means be accomplished. For quite some time to come the problems of our friends here and on the Continent will call for all our strength and attention.

SWITZERLAND REVISES REFUGEE POLICY

Swiss policy towards refugees is expected to undergo far-reaching changes as a result of a recent conference of the heads of cantonal police departments. The conference unanimously approved a draft decree of the Federal Authorities providing for the grant of permanent residence in Switzerland to elderly refugees. It was also decided to issue labour permits to most of the refugees now in Switzerland, provided that they do not impair the interests of Swiss citizens. At the same time, the conference expressed the wish that from time to time refugees should be obliged to enlist in the Land Army in order to relieve the acute shortage of farm hands.

Private relief agencies must care for about 14,000 elderly or sick refugees, children and Stateless persons.

THE HYPHEN

formed in 1948 by a number of young people from the Continent who,
having settled in Great Britain, found that owing to their similar
background and experiences, they had interests and problems in
common which justified the formation of a Group without a particular
religious or political bias, to provide for cultural, social and
welfare activities.

H-H-H-H-H-H-H-H-H-H

CONSTITUTION OF THE HYPHEN

1. **Membership**
   Membership is open to persons over 21 years of age who are in
agreement with the aims and general character of the Group, and whose
application for membership has the support of two members, subject to
the approval of the Committee (c.f.5).

2. **General Meetings**
   There shall be a General Meeting in March of every year. The
quorum shall consist of one quarter of the number of paid-up members.
All motions shall be duly proposed and seconded, and voted upon by
simple majority PROVIDED ONLY that matters affecting the Constitution
and major policy shall require a two-thirds majority. Of these
written notice should be given by the Secretary.
   A General Meeting may also be called at any time by the Committee
after having given notice five weeks in advance and must be called
within three months of receipt by the Secretary of a written demand
for a General Meeting signed by ten members. Three weeks' notice
of a General Meeting shall be given to all members and the agenda
circulated in advance. Procedure at a General Meeting is at the
discretion of the Chairman or his Deputy.

3. **Elections and Committee**
   Election of Committee Members shall take place at the Annual
General Meeting in March as follows:-
   Candidates shall be nominated by two members in writing to the
Secretary before February 1st and their names circulates to all
members. If less than six nominations have been received by
the 1st February, additional nominations can be made from the
floor at the A.G.M. At the General Meeting every member shall
have six votes and the six candidates heading the vote shall be
deemed elected Committee Members.
   The six elected Committee Members shall choose the Chairman from
amongst themselves. It is left to the discretion of the elected
Committee to co-opt additional members during their turn of office
but so as not to exceed a total of nine Committee Members. The
Committee shall choose the Secretary and Treasurer from amongst
themselves and the complete composition of the new Committee shall

be circulated to all members together with the addresses of the Secretary and Treasurer within four weeks of the Annual General Meeting.

The Chairman shall call a Special General Meeting of The Hyphen if more than three elected members of the Committee have resigned.

4. Finances

The Group shall be non-profit making and the rate of subscription shall be fixed by the Committee in accordance with views expressed by members at the Annual General Meeting. The Treasurer shall present a Statement of Accounts to the Annual General Meeting.

5. Special Contingencies

Matters arising out of resignation of Committee members, alterations of subscription, waiving of the rule regarding two Supporters for the application of prospective members, and matters of a similar nature shall be dealt with at the discretion of the Committee.

H-H-H-H-H-H-H-H-H-H-H-H

The Hyphen was founded in 1948 by Peter Johnson, a German Jewish refugee, and a group of younger Jewish refugees between the ages of 20 and 35, many of whom were the children of AJR members. Having settled in Britain, Hyphen members found that because of their similar experiences, they had many interests and challenges in common. It was named 'The Hyphen' because it symbolised the gap between the older generation of refugees and a younger generation that aimed to integrate seamlessly into British society. The group had no particular religious or political bent, and was intended to offer cultural, social and welfare activities.

Constitution of The Hyphen, c. late 1940s.

A life somewhere else

After being forced to leave, Jewish refugees who managed to reach Britain had to adjust to a new country whose language and culture was not their own.

Many refugees benefited from the help of organisations as well as generous individuals. However, the obstacles they faced – adapting to new, not always sympathetic surroundings and coping with the loss of family, profession, and homeland – were tremendous.

Moreover, Britain was at war, and refugees endured shortages and bombings like other residents. Jewish refugees lacked extensive personal networks, and unlike Polish or Czech refugees, they did not have national representation by a government-in-exile. Nearer to the end of the war, they were uncertain about whether they could or should stay in Britain. The overwhelming majority of Jewish refugees who came before the war became naturalised citizens after war's end and attempted to pick up the pieces of their lives. While many settled in London, other cities such as Manchester, Oxford, Cambridge, Leeds and Glasgow also received refugees.

'I've been working as a waitress in Lyons for the last two weeks, earning anything between two to four pounds a week, which means I'm getting by quite well. Apart from work I hardly see anyone nowadays. I stay home and don't want to go out anymore...I'm beginning to feel very disappointed with life. The last few years haven't brought me any happy memories. Nothing much nice has happened in my youth.'

Ilse Shatkin (née Gruenwald), A young Jewish refugee, 21 January 1942 diary entry

Loss and Hope

The circumstances of emigration shaped Jewish refugee communities in Britain. Because of entry requirements, many Jewish refugees in Britain were professionals, scholars or well-known artists with resources to emigrate and networks to obtain visas and sponsors. Couples without children and younger people were able to emigrate more easily than the elderly and poor.

Child refugees, separated from their parents and sent on the *Kindertransport*, faced particular challenges. They were dependent on the generosity of strangers and more susceptible to abuse or exploitation. Older children and adolescents placed in youth hostels found some camaraderie, but were still separated abruptly from the familiar. Both men and women coped with poverty and the loss of their professional lives, taking on menial labour to scrape by. Thousands of women who came as domestic servants, often with little or no training,

were underpaid, sometimes maltreated, and subject to hostility and class discrimination. In many refugee families, women stepped into the breach and became the main breadwinner, adapting to jobs as cooks and cleaners, as men were sometimes not allowed to practice their previous professions in Britain.

Many organisations continued their relief work and support of refugees, including newly arriving survivors, well after the war ended. The contributions of Jewish refugees to the arts, medicine, science, and industry have been numerous. In general, Jewish refugees integrated into British society, although for some this was more difficult or even impossible. A minority of Jewish refugees left Britain for the United States, Palestine and elsewhere. That the great majority chose to remain indicates that they were able to see a future for themselves in Britain, despite the extreme hardships of their early years here.

Purim Party at the Beacon
Rustal Refugee Home near
Tunbridge Wells, 1940

Weir Courtney was one of several hostels that received child survivors after the war. A government scheme proposed by the Jewish Refugee Committee permitted 1,000 children to enter Britain for recuperation; in the end, 732 children came.

Two child survivors of the Holocaust, Eva (left) and Hanna Taub, at the Weir Courtney Hostel, Lingfield, 1946-7.

FELLOW REFUGEES

Sir,—*Walking up St. Marylebone High Street the other day I met some fellow refugees. They were resting in a little church garden, just off the road, and on a tombstone that stood out, it said: " The Burial Place of Claude Champion de Crespigny. A Refugee from France. Died on April 10, 1697. Also of his Wife, Marie de Vierville. Died on June 21, 1708." I thought of the many who rest in Hoop Lane and in Willesden, and as I saluted the Huguenot couple, across 250 years, the lines of Byron came into my mind :—*

> " But we must wander witheringly
> In other lands to die;
> And where our fathers' ashes be
> Our own may never lie."

Yours faithfully,

Aaron Casper.

Letter to the editor, May 1955, *AJR Information*

A 'Winton Child': Gerda Mayer

In 2005, Mayer published an autobiographical book of poetry and prose. Prague Winter, Hearing Eye, 2005.

Gerda Mayer (née Stein), born in 1927 in Karlsbad (in then Czechoslovakia), fled with her family to Prague in 1938, just before Nazi Germany annexed the Sudetenland. Her parents tried valiantly to find a way to emigrate. In February 1939, Gerda's father, Arnold, asked for help from Trevor Chadwick, an Englishman who was assisting rescue operations organised by Doreen Warriner and Sir Nicholas Winton. Warriner worked to smuggle out political refugees (including many Jews) illegally, and Winton arranged for the emigration of Jewish children, organising their reception and care upon arrival in England. Trevor Chadwick remained in Prague until June 1939, managing the departure of the children, including Mayer. For a time, Mayer stayed with the Chadwick family and later became a naturalised British citizen and a published poet.

NEW DITTON
PINKNEY'S GREEN
MAIDENHEAD
SL6 6NT
MAIDENHEAD 26613

28.3.99.

Dear Gerda,

I am delighted to hear that at long last Trevor Chadwick may possibly get full recognition for the part he played in saving children from Czechoslovakia prior to the 2nd world war.

I saw the need when I was in Prague just after Christmas 38/(. Trevor came out and offered his help and we set up an office together and he agreed to run the Czech side, if, on my return to England, I was able to make workable arrangements withe the Home Office. This I was able to do and my job then was to find suitable families which fulfilled the Home Office conditions of entry. Trevor then went to work and dealt with all the considerable problems at the Prague end and thisa work he continued to carry on evdn when it became more difficult and dangeerous when the Germans arrived. He deserves all praise.

greetings, Nicky Winton

Letter dated 28 March 1999 from Sir Nicholas Winton to Gerda Mayer about his work with Trevor Chadwick

Lilli Goldwerth was born in Vienna in 1922. Her parents, Abraham and Franziska, tried to make arrangements for her to emigrate to England in 1939. En route, she was to stay with her father's employer, Captain Geoffrey Austin, in St Andrews, Scotland. However, Abraham and Franziska Goldwerth were obliged to leave their daughter behind as her visa did not arrive in time. The couple reached Britain in August 1939 with domestic permits. Lilli's visa was later cancelled because of the outbreak of the war. In 1942, her parents were informed via a Red Cross letter that their daughter had died in Vienna on 20 March 1941. Abraham and Franziska Goldwerth became British by naturalisation in 1949.

Lilli Goldwerth's passport.

PERSONENBESCHREIBUNG

		Ehefrau
Beruf	Schülerin	
Geburtsort	Wien	
Geburtstag	8. II. 1922	
Wohnort	Wien	
Gestalt	mittel	
Gesicht	oval	
Farbe der Augen	braun	
Farbe des Haares	braun	
Besond. Kennzeichen	/	

KINDER

Name	Alter	Geschlecht

e durch
ist und
lig voll-

9

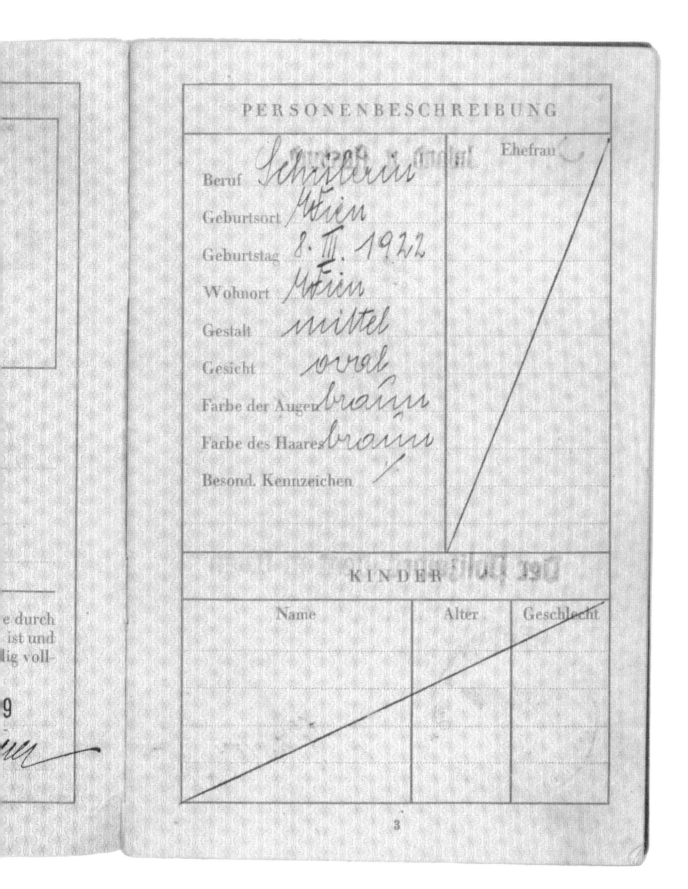

Nummer 1

UNSERE ZEITUNG

i n

UNSEREM HEIM

Zwölf Kinder aus Deutschland - Acht-bis Zwölfjäh-
rige- haben durch den Gemeinschaftssinn ihrer Mitmenschen
ein Heim gefunden. Die Zwölf sind verschieden in ihrem Cha-
rakter und ihren Lebensgewohnheiten. Aber es gibt etwas, das
sie zusammenführt und zusammenhält: die Gemeinschaft ihres
jetzigen Lebens. Dass sie in diese Gemeinschaft hinein-
wachsen, zeigen ihre Aeusserungen in "Unsere Zeitung in
unserem Heim."
Unsere Zeitung soll alle vier Wochen erscheinen und
die Kinder, Eltern und Freunde unseres Heims an unserem
Leben und unserer Entwicklung teilnehmen lassen.

Wir machen unsere Zeitung.

Hostels for young refugees were opened by
organisations and individuals, often with support
from local churches and synagogues. In March 1939,
Bernard Schlesinger, a prominent paediatrician, and
his wife, Winifred – both immigrants from Germany
with five children of their own – opened a hostel
in Highgate for twelve children. They housed a
thirteenth refugee child in their own home. The
hostel operated until September 1939, when it was
evacuated due to the war.

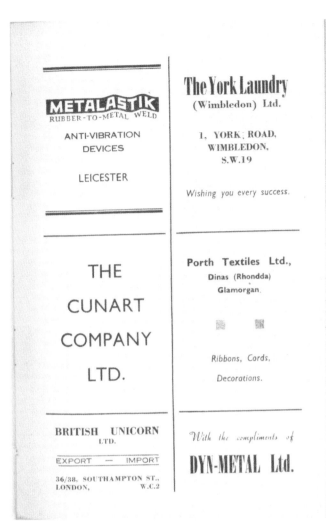

This publication by the AJR features advertisements from dozens of firms, many of which were founded by Jewish refugees. The firms included textile companies, metal merchants, chemical and fabric manufacturers.

A page of advertisements from *Dispersion and Resettlement: the story of the Jews from Central Europe*, by Werner Rosenstock, AJR: 1955.

Photo of Ruth Ucko, undated.

Marriage announcement
of Ruth Ucko and Edward
Thomas Shellard, 1947.

1651/1/36

Ruth Ucko

and

Edward Thomas Shellard

announce their Marriage

in London.

25. Meadway,
Laleham Road,
Staines. Middlesex.   December. 1947.

Ruth Ucko, born in Breslau in 1914, emigrated to England in 1939, where she worked as a childminder, a nurse and later in the fashion industry. As a young child, Ruth had been adopted, and her adoptive parents had died before she came to England. She maintained close contact with her biological mother, Frieda Wolzendorff, whom she helped emigrate to England after Frieda had been imprisoned in Lichtenburg and then released. Ruth's diary is opened to the first page that appears in English (prior to this date, Ruth wrote in German). It reads: 'I am very happy today as after a long time of loneliness I am about to get married and have a wonderful companion for life.' Ruth Ucko died in Brighton in 2002.

Diary of Ruth Ucko (1939-1947).

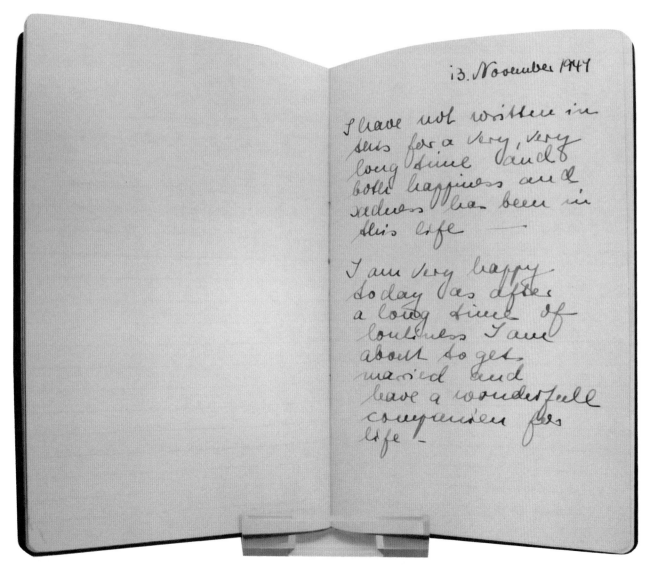

Serving to survive: Domestic servant refugees in focus

Before the war, a third of all Jewish refugees – more than 20,000 women – came to Britain on visas granted for domestic service. British Government policy in this regard was both opportunistic and humanitarian: it aimed to fill a gap in the labour force whilst also recognising that the women, who were often middle class and had no formal training, would likely not remain in these positions.

Jewish women determined eligible for domestic service visas were placed in both Jewish and non-Jewish homes across Britain, a process administered by Bloomsbury House. In some homes, they were treated well, but in many cases they were exploited and their wages were meagre. Their employers often showed little sympathy for their circumstances as refugees. After the German invasion of Poland, suspicion about 'enemy aliens' at home prompted widespread dismissals of refugee domestics and some were interned. During the war, many happily found work elsewhere and contributed to the British war effort.

Despite these hardships, refugee domestic servants were resilient. They became the main breadwinners of their families, separated from spouses and children, whose fates sometimes remained unknown to them. They created networks of support and campaigned for better work conditions, with little to no trade union help.

'I cannot think with affection of the time I spent as a domestic.'
Marion Smith

MISTRESS AND MAID

*General Information for the use
of Domestic Refugees and their
Employers.*

Issued by :

THE DOMESTIC BUREAU,
Central Office for Refugees,
Bloomsbury House,
Bloomsbury Street,
London, W.C.1   APRIL, 1940

Mistress and Maid

THE LEGAL POSITION AND HOUSEHOLD CUSTOMS

EMPLOYMENT. Permission must be obtained by the *mistress* from her local Ministry of Labour Employment Exchange to employ a refugee placed in Class " C " by the Tribunal. The name of a specific refugee must be given when making the application.

Permission must be obtained from the Home Office before any refugee placed in Class " B " by the Tribunal may be employed. The Domestic Bureau or the Local Committee are prepared to act on behalf of the employer.

Under no circumstances may any domestic refugee proceed to her new post before such permission is granted, either by the local Employment Exchange or by the Home Office.

WAGES. The wages must be approved by the Employment Exchange or the Home Office, whichever the case may be. Wages and other conditions of service must be equal to those enjoyed by British subjects of the same age in the district for similar work.

BREAKAGES. Breakages cannot be deducted from wages, even where gross negligence can be proved, but if the maid offers to pay for breakage and requests the employer to deduct it from her wages, then the employer is entitled to deduct it, but it is proper for the employer to pay the wages in full and for the servant to tender the amount for breakage.

3

Mistress and Maid pamphlet, produced by Bloomsbury House, suggested to the reader: 'Adapt yourself as quickly as possible to your new surroundings.'

1 Holmbury View
CLAPTON E. 5.

LONDON ENGLAND

24. 2. 39

Dear Miss Mandl,

The Refugee committe herein London have given
me your name and adress and also various particulars of
your qualifications and I understand that you are prepared
to come here into domestic service. I am quite willing to
engage you provided that you are prepared to carry out the
duties required. We are a family of 6 persons, (5 adults and
a boy of 12 years.) The work will include a little washing
of clothes, cleaning of dishes and general housework. You
will have no cooking to do, but there will be light housework
on Saturday . You will be assured of a good comfortable home,
good outings and will be treated like a member of the family.

I am quite sure that you will be happy here provided
that you are perfectly clear in your mind what you will
have to do. I am quite willing to assist you if you are
prepared to do the rough work.

I have signed the various documents but please
write me by return telling what experience you have had
in general housework and whether you thaink you will
care to work for me.

We all understand Jewish here.

Yours truly

Mrs. S. Hurst.

Letter from Mrs S Hurst to Miss Frieda Mandel (then Newton), dated 24 February 1939. Frieda Mandel was born in Vatra Dornei, Romania, on 20 April 1916 and grew up in Vienna. She came to England in 1939 as a domestic servant and recalled that she was poorly treated.

JEWISH REFUGEES COMMITTEE

Telephone : MUSeum 6811
Cables: "Refugees, Westcent, London"

*In your reply please quote
the reference given below*

BLOOMSBURY HOUSE
BLOOMSBURY STREET
LONDON,   W.C.1

TRA/HP/CF 120210

6th January, 1948.

Mrs. F. Newton,
86, Kilburn High Road,
N.W.6.

Dear Mrs. Newton,

    With reference to your enquiry for Jakob and Regina Rachel Mandel, we are very sorry to let you know that your mother was deported to Theresienstadt on the 24th September, 1942.   Mr. Jankel Mandel, born 10.7.1880, was deported to Izbica on the 12th May, 1942.

    We are very sorry indeed that we are not in a position to let you have better news.

Yours sincerely,

(Miss) M. Bloch

TRACING DEPARTMENT.

Letter from the Jewish
Refugees Committee to
Frieda Newton (née Mandel),
6 January 1948, regarding
the result of her search for
her parents

The Media and Forced Migration

Both the displacement of people as a consequence of war and atrocity and representations of refugees as 'floods' are increasingly commonplace. The headlines are familiar. So too is the range of humanitarian interventions and governmental responses routinely triggered by mass movements of people.

Patterns in media discourse and representation from the past and present often categorise refugees and migration, distinguishing between those who are 'deserving' and 'eligible', and those who are not. A symbiosis between media and policy contributes to the perception of migration and immigration as crisis: a perpetual, intractable problem. Policy is transmitted to media, whose stories, often shared rapidly via social media, then feed back into policy. This cycle encourages a 'language' of migration. It is this language, with its use of dehumanising and anaesthetised terms, that often has the power to corrupt thought and action.

This exhibition raises important questions: why do some waves of migration elicit sympathy, whilst others generate hostility? What insight can we gain into the shortcomings of humanitarian, national and popular responses? What are the lessons – if any – from history?

'But if thought corrupts language, language can also corrupt thought. A bad usage can spread by tradition and imitation even among people who should and do know better.'

George Orwell, "Politics and the English Language", 1946

© Carl Lutz, Budapest, 1944

© Daily Herald, 1938

© Nóra Bartóki-Gönczy, 2015

Ahmad al-Rashid:
A voice for refugees

In 2015, twenty-five-year old Ahmad al-Rashid, who was born in Aleppo, Syria, joined thousands of others who made the difficult decision to embark on a dangerous journey, first by sea, then by treacherous border crossings, to flee war-torn Syria. Al-Rashid has recalled that he is amongst the lucky ones who survived and reached safer ground, but thousands of others did not: 'Thousands of these desperate souls were lost for the sea, these souls' tragedy became headlines for a couple of days and they were forgotten, [although] their memories will not be forgotten by their loved ones.'

Al-Rashid arrived in the UK after a 55-day-long journey in difficult circumstances, which included hiding in the back of a lorry after spending nearly two weeks in Calais. Whilst he was relieved to finally reach Britain, he admits that 'it wasn't an easy start…imagine yourself arriving in a new country and everything you have is only the clothes you are putting on.' While he waited to be granted asylum by the UK Government, he relied upon charities and generous individuals to find housing and support. One organisation, Refugees at Home, linked him with a host family that provided him a room for four months in Surrey. After surmounting many bureaucratic hurdles, he managed to bring his family from Syria to Britain on a family reunion visa.

Since his arrival in the UK, al-Rashid has been working with various groups and organisations advocating for refugee rights. He has spoken in the UK Parliament on several occasions and appeared on the BBC, ITV, Zagros and other media outlets and has participated in panels, events and public debates to raise awareness about the plight of Syrian refugees. He is currently a postgraduate student at SOAS, University of London studying violence, conflict and development.

Ahmad al-Rashid with Lord Alf Dubs, who came to England on the *Kindertransport*, and who is a prominent campaigner for refugees. © Ahmad al-Rashid

Epilogue

History makes a frequent appearance in today's media coverage and popular discourse about forced migration and Britain's responses, potential and actual, to refugees. Britain is cast as having been historically open to refugees and immigration, a tradition many hope policymakers will uphold as the fates of millions of refugees from Syria, Iraq, Afghanistan, Somalia and elsewhere remain in the balance.

The *Kindertransport* is frequently cited as a successful scheme by the British government to save child refugees during the Nazi period. Yet the arrival of thousands of Jewish children could not have been carried out without financial and other support from charitable and religious organisations and private individuals - the government waived visa restrictions for the children, yet support for the children had to be organised privately. And although the lives of the *Kinder* were spared, many left behind families whose visas were never approved and who, in the end, perished in the Holocaust.

Our starting point for this exhibition was to critically examine British responses to the displacement of people in the 1930s and 1940s, putting schemes like the *Kindertransport* in context. In considering continuities with the past, our driving question for the exhibition has been: what was distinctive about the experiences of and responses to Jewish and other refugees in Britain in the 1930s and 1940s? Our exploration led us to assess critically the various responses to the refugee crisis at the international level, by the British government and also by individuals and groups. What worked and how? What were the shortcomings and failures? And how did refugees cope with the bureaucratic and logistical hurdles to reach life in a new country, to a language and culture that was not their own?

While one section of the exhibition looks back, the other focuses on the present. It is our hope that by thinking critically about the past, visitors may be better informed about and prepared to respond to the present refugee crisis faced in Britain, Europe and globally. Some aspects, particularly historical context, are different. Others, specifically the fear and hope experienced by refugees as they made and continue to make their way to Britain, remain strikingly and painfully familiar.

Dr Christine Schmidt, Deputy Director and Head of Research

Christine Schmidt holds a doctorate in History from Clark University, a post-graduate certificate in Museum Studies from The George Washington University and a bachelor's degree from the University of Michigan-Dearborn. Her research has focused on rescue and resistance in Vichy France and Hungary and the Nazi concentration camp system.

Dr Barbara Warnock, Education and Outreach Manager

Barbara Warnock holds a doctorate in History from Birkbeck College, University of London, where she also obtained her Master's degree in European History. She also holds a Post-Graduate Certificate in Education, and was a history teacher for many years. She has published A-Level revision textbooks, and her academic research has focussed on the political, social, economic and financial crisis in Austria in the early 1920s, and international responses to this.

Sources

1: Overview
Hans Kohl Austrian Centre card, WL 1685;
Eva Kolmer, Landesarchiv Berlin; Map, The Red
Cross and the Refugees, United Nations High
Commissioner for Refugees; Neuhaus letter and
photo, WL 1718/3/1-51; Photograph, 'Deportation of
the Jews', WL Photo Archive, Box 45.1

2: Official solutions
Rothschild papers, WL 1802; Photo: Martha
Rothschild, Yad Vashem; Photo: Internees on Isle
of Man, WL Photo Archive 8139, Behrend papers,
WL1690/4/59; Simon papers, WL2016/41; Steiner
papers, WL 1827/5

3: International responses
Photo: British Red Cross Staff, WL Photo Archive
4558, Wirth papers, courtesy of David Wirth and ITS
Digital Archive, Wiener Library; Red Cross telegram
instructions, WL1802; Josephs Red Cross telegrams,
WL 1329/69-83

4: My brother's keeper
Lewin papers, WL645; The Hyphen Club
Constitution, WL1159; While You are in England,
WL1685; Bloomsbury House table, WL863

5: A life somewhere else
Mayer papers, WL1809; Ucko papers, WL1651;
Shlesinger hostel papers, WL1625; Goldwerth
papers, WL1825

6: Serving to survive
Newton papers and domestic service application,
WL1786

7: Image by Carl Lutz, WL7215, Young girl on the
Kindertransport, WL 30. The following images
are available under the (CC) Creative Commons
Attribution-ShareAlike 4.0 International License:
https://creativecommons.org/licenses/by-sa/4.0/
deed.en.

Image by Nóra Bartóki-Gönczy, 2015
Image by Mstyslav Chernov, 2015
Image by Rebecca Harms, 2015

Additional sources consulted

Baumel-Schwartz, Judy Tydor. *Never look back: the Jewish refugee children in Great Britain 1938-1945.* West Lafayette: Purdue University, 2012.

Bolchover, Richard. *British Jewry and the Holocaust.* Oxford: Littman Library of Jewish Civilization, 2003.

Cohen, Susan. *Rescue the Perishing: Eleanor Rathbone and the Refugees.* London: Vallentine Mitchell, 2010.

Dwork, Debórah and Robert Jan van Pelt. *Flight from the Reich: Refugee Jews, 1933-1946.* London: Norton, 2009.

Grenville, Anthony. "The Association of Jewish Refugees". http://www.ajr.org.uk/documents/ Exile_10_05_-_Anthony_Grenville.pdf (accessed 6 October 2016).

Grenville, Anthony. *Jewish Refugees from Germany and Austria in Britain, 1933-1970.* London: Vallentine Mitchell, 2010.

Grenville, Anthony and Andrea Reiter, eds. *Political Exile and Exile Politics in Britain after 1933.* Amsterdam: Rodopi, 2011.

Kirkwood, S. et al. The Language of Asylum: Refugees and Discourse. Palgrave Macmillan, 2016.

Kushner, Tony. "An Alien Occupation -- Jewish Refugees and Domestic Service in Britain, 1933-1948" in *Second Chance: Two Centuries of German-speaking Jews in the United Kingdom.* Tuebingen: Mohr, 1991, 553-578.

Kushner, Tony. *The Battle of Britishness: Migrant Journeys, 1685 to the Present.* Manchester: Manchester University Press, 2012.

London, Louise. *Whitehall and the Jews, 1933-1948: British Immigration Policy, Jewish Refugees and the Holocaust.* Cambridge: Cambridge University Press, 2003.

London, Louise. 'Whitehall and the refugees: the 1930s and the 1990s', in *Patterns of Prejudice* 34, no. 3 (July 2000), 17-26.

Reinisch, Jessica and Matthew Frank. "Refugees and the Nation-State in Europe 1919-1959." *Journal of Contemporary History Special Edition* 49, no. 3 (July 2014): 477-490.

Reinisch, Jessica. "History matters… but which one? Every refugee crisis has a context." *History & Policy,* 29 September 2015.

Stent, Ronald. "Jewish Refugee Organisations" in Second Chance: Two Centuries of *German-speaking Jews in the United Kingdom.* Tuebingen: Mohr, 1991, 579-598.

Stone, Dan. *The Liberation of the Camps: the End of the Holocaust and its Aftermath.* London: Yale University Press, 2015.

Acknowledgements

With special thanks to Imogen Bayley, Yvonne Bernstein, Esme Chandler, Kitty Cooper, Judith Fixler, Brian Goldfarb, Anthony Grenville, Susanne Samson, Paul Sinclair, Melvyn Tymel and all of the Wiener Library's supporters who have donated and made this exhibition and catalogue possible.

Made in the USA
Columbia, SC
27 May 2018